Pathfinder - Career Guidance By Experts

Confused? Don't know where your career is heading? Relax!

Oucareers | Career Guidance, Career Advice & Counseling,

-Vikas Srivastava

Index

How to Find a Career Mentor

A career mentor is someone who shares their knowledge and expertise with you in order to help you set goals, fix problems, and make good choices along your career path. I have been privileged to have career mentors who have helped me throughout my career.

The first was my supervisor many years ago, He taught me just about everything I know about business and about communicating effectively with people. He also helped me move up the career ladder at our company, helped me job search, and continued to provide advice when I moved on.

Another person who mentored me is someone with vast experience writing about careers. When she and I first met, I had recently transitioned from Human Resources and she shared her advice and wisdom. Over the years, she has also helped promote my expertise, my books, and my other work. I wouldn't be where I am today without their assistance.

A good career mentor, just like my mentors, voluntarily provides that career advice and assistance. The relationship you'll have with your mentor will be ongoing and your mentor can guide you throughout the life of your career. It's a relationship that can last a very long time. A mentor can be indispensable both when you're starting out and when you're moving up the career ladder.

Who and How to Ask for Help

Perhaps the most important step in pursuing a dream job is to find someone who already works in that field who can offer guidance and advice as you proceed. I know that sounds intimidating, but it doesn't have to be. Believe it or not, this is not as difficult as it might sound.

In my experience, many people express fear at the prospect of asking for help from a prospective mentor who may a total stranger. Why would they want to help you, after all? The answer is easy: people like helping other people!

By asking a prospective mentor for help, you're essentially letting them know they are admired for what they do and that their career is in demand. It's a good feeling and many people want to know their experiences and insights are valuable to others.

It's not universal, of course, and not everyone will see it this way. You may run into a person who think might be a mentorship candidate who doesn't care what people think and isn't interested in helping you along your career path. But, you'll see, once you start asking, you'll be surprised at just how receptive many people are.

Of course, not all mentor candidates will be strangers. You may have a former boss, professor, or your family members or friends may know of someone who may be able to help you.

Tips for Finding a Good Career Mentor

Even with a few words of encouragement, the idea of searching for and finding a career mentor may seem scary, so here are a few tips to you get you started:

- If you're brand new or changing careers, it may be a good idea to research the field and find out about the top people who are in it.
- Learn what you can about their background, education, and even common interests.
- Create a list of people who seem like they might be good fits for you and your career goals.
- Start contacting the people on your list but go slowly with each one. Start with a polite and formal email to introduce yourself and see who responds.
- Be patient – your potential mentor candidates may be busy, and it could take a day or two for any of them to respond.
- Try to form a relationship with them and get to know their personalities even as you try to exhibit yours. Like so many other things, when you find the right mentor, you'll know it.

The guidance and advice from a good career mentor may be just what you need to guide you through your next set of career steps. Good luck and who knows? Maybe someday someone will be contacting you to be their mentor.

Elevator Pitch Examples and Writing Tips

What's an elevator pitch, and how can it help your career? An elevator pitch (which is also called an elevator speech) is a quick synopsis of your background and experience. The reason it's called an elevator speech is that you should be able to present it during a brief elevator ride. Done right, this short speech helps you introduce yourself to career connections in a compelling way.

Section 2

What's In an Elevator Pitch?

This speech is all about you: who you are, what you do, and what you want to do (if you're job hunting).

Your elevator pitch is a way to share your expertise and credentials quickly and effectively with people who don't know you.

Read on for guidelines for what to include in your speech, when to share it, and examples of elevator pitches.

When and How to Use an Elevator Speech

If you're job searching, you can use your elevator pitch at job fairs and career expos, and online in your LinkedIn summary or Twitter bio, for example. An elevator speech is a great way to gain confidence in introducing yourself to hiring managers and company representatives.

You can also use your elevator pitch to introduce yourself at networking events and mixers. If you're attending professional association programs and events, or any other type of gathering, have your pitch ready to share with those you meet.

Your elevator pitch can be used during job interviews, especially when you're asked about yourself. Interviewers often begin with the question, "Tell me about yourself" — think of your elevator pitch as a super-condensed version of your response to that request.

What to Say

Your elevator speech should be brief. Restrict the speech to 30 to 60 seconds — that's the time it takes to ride an elevator, hence the name. You don't need to include your entire work history and career objectives.

You need to be persuasive. Even though it's a short pitch, your elevator speech should be persuasive enough to spark the listener's interest in your idea, organization, or background.

Share your skills. Your elevator pitch should explain who you are and what qualifications and skills you have. Try to focus on assets that add value in many situations. This is your chance to brag a bit — avoid sounding boastful but do share what you bring to the table.

Practice, practice, practice. The best way to get comfortable with an elevator speech is to practice it until the speed and "pitch" come naturally, without sounding robotic. You will become comfortable varying the conversation as you practice with it.

Try saying your speech to a friend, or record it. This will help you know if you are staying within the time limit and giving a coherent message.

Be flexible. You aren't interviewing for a specific position, so you want to appear open-minded and flexible. It's your chance to make a great first impression with a potential employer.

Mention your goals. You don't need to get too specific. An overly targeted goal isn't helpful since your pitch will be used in many circumstances, and with many different types of people. But do remember to say what you're looking for. For instance, you might say, "a role in accounting" or "an opportunity to apply my sales skills to a new market" or "to relocate to San Francisco with a job in this same industry."

Know your audience, and speak to them. In some cases, using jargon can be a powerful move — it demonstrates your industry knowledge. But be wary of using jargon during an elevator pitch, particularly if you're speaking to recruiters, who may find the terms unfamiliar and off-putting.

Have a business card ready. If you have a business card, offer it at the end of the conversation as a way to continue the dialog. A copy of your resume, if you're at a job fair or professional networking event, will also show your enthusiasm and preparedness.

What Not to Say and Do During Your Elevator Speech

Don't speak too fast. Yes, you only have a short time to convey a lot of information. But don't try to fix this dilemma by speaking quickly. This will just make it hard for listeners to absorb your message.

Avoid rambling. Therefore, it's so important to practice your elevator speech.

While you don't want to over-rehearse, and subsequently sound stilted, you also don't want to have unfocused or unclear sentences in your pitch or get off-track.

Don't frown, or speak in a monotone. Here's one of the downsides to rehearsing: it can leave you more focused on remembering the exact words you want to use, and less on how you're carrying yourself. Keep your energy level high, positive, and enthusiastic.

Modulate your voice to keep listeners interested, and keep your facial expression friendly.

Don't restrict yourself to a single elevator pitch. Maybe you're interested in pursuing two fields — public relations and content strategy. Many of your communication skills will apply to both those fields, but you'll want to tailor your pitch depending on who you are speaking to. You may also want to have a more casual, personal pitch prepared for social settings.

Section 3

What You Need to Know — And Do — If You Received a Warning at Work

Typically, warnings ratchet up. First, your boss may informally tell you that there's a problem. The next step is either a verbal or written warning, both of which are documented. This is a more formal action, and can involve human resources. If the behavior is not addressed, termination of employment is typically the next step after verbal and/or written warnings.

Here's what you need to know about what it means to receive a warning at work, and how to respond when you receive one, whether it's verbal or written.

What It Means to Get a Warning

Many people work under "at-will employment," which means they're free to resign at any point. It also means the company can also terminate employment for any reason. Still, even when companies have the freedom to terminate an employee without providing a reason, few opt to do so. For one thing, companies can potentially open themselves up to a lawsuit if an employee believes there was discrimination behind the termination. And, perhaps just as importantly, morale throughout a company can suffer if people are let go for no reason.

Instead, most companies have a policy in place to govern how poor behavior or work will be dealt with. Often, this is referred to as progressive discipline – the idea is that warnings will escalate from a conversation to verbal or written warnings. For both verbal and written warnings, there is typically a formal meeting and written documentation that is added to your employee folder. Often, both your supervisor and human resources will attend.

Note: Warnings are serious business, not to be mistaken with being chewed out by your supervisor. You can think of a warning as an early step in the termination process.

If you receive a warning, does it mean you will be fired or let go? Not necessarily. It's possible you will change your behavior or work in a way that satisfies your manager. Still, it is a very serious action for your manager to take, and one that shows deep dissatisfaction with your performance. Even if you are resolved to rectify any errors and stay with the company, it may be wise to consider updating your resume and LinkedIn and preparing for a job search.

How to Respond to a Warning

Receiving a warning can feel surprising, devastating, and often unfair. How should you respond? There is no one correct answer, of course, but here are some guidelines to follow:

Stay calm: During the meeting to discuss your warning, and afterwards, do your very best to avoid crying, raising your voice, or showing extreme distress. This may, of course, be easier said than done.

Take notes: It can help that first goal — keeping calm — to take notes during any meeting about the warning. Also, this will help you remember precisely what was said. Important points to get down are why you are receiving the warning and what actions you can take going forward to rectify the situation.

Make your case: Do you disagree with your warning? If you feel comfortable doing so, you can speak up during the meeting to make your case and defend yourself. This is a tricky situation — you want to defend yourself, but not seem defensive. That's not easy!

Avoid getting personal or comparing yourself to other employees in heated tones, which can seem childish.

Do defend yourself on the spot if you feel comfortable doing so, but know you can also remain quiet in the moment and give yourself time to assemble your thoughts and respond later.

Ask what you can do differently: Before you leave the meeting or sign any acknowledgment of a warning, you'll want to be sure you understand a) precisely what you did wrong, and b) the correct behavior going forward. Sometimes this can be very straight-forward.

For instance, if you are receiving a warning for being late to work 10 times in a one-month period, and your boss says you cannot be late for the next four weeks. Other times, a warning may be about something a bit more nebulous. For example, you may be faulted for having a "bad attitude" or "not being engaged with a project." In those situations, you'll want to make sure that a plan is clearly laid out for what would constitute improving in those areas.

Follow up with a written rebuttal: Do you feel your warning is unmerited? As well as making a case in your meeting, you can also write a written rebuttal letter. In your letter, you should make a case to defend yourself. For instance, if you were late to work, but you'd requested and received permission to do so, print out those emails from your supervisor. Again, for less clear-cut infractions, defending yourself is trickier.

Take some time to reflect: It's only human to respond to criticism by defending yourself. But do take some time to think about the facts and comments in the warning. Are any of them justified? Consider what you could possibly do differently.

Try to figure out if the warning is the last step, or a turnaround point: Sometimes warnings are issued as a way for the employer to protect themselves from a lawsuit prior to a termination. But that's not always the case. Sometimes, your supervisor or human resources department genuinely believe the situation can be fixed. Do your best to figure out the spirit in which your warning was given.

Follow up with your manager: During meetings with your manager, ask for feedback. This will help give you a sense of your next steps.

Ideally, you'll have concrete goals or steps to improve your work/behavior.

Start a job search: Finally, it's wise to start making moves to kick off your job search. Again, a warning does not necessarily mean you will be terminated. But it is a possibility. Consider networking, reaching out to former co-workers to see if they know of any job openings, updating your resume, and applying to jobs.

Section 4

10 Skills to Work in Information Technology

Whether you are just starting your technical career or looking to make a career change, it helps to know what career skills are hot in the job market. The following list is of technical skills that are currently in high demand. The list includes information, a brief history of each technology, and links to training resources.

1. Unix Operating System

The Unix Operating System is the foundation of the internet. Unix is a critical skill for a career in Information Technology.

2. Linux Operating System

The Linux Operating System is a Unix-like operating system that is being used by many large companies. It is quickly growing in popularity and is a popular operating system to develop for. Linux is a great career skill if you want a career as a System Administrator.

3. Java Programming Language

Java is an object-oriented programming language developed by Sun Micro systems. Java is a popular career skill if you want to be a Web Developer.

4. C++ Programming Language

C++ is another high level, object-oriented programming language. C++ is often used in commercial application software development. It has been and continues to be a hot programming career skill in the market. A career as a Software Engineer would be the most likely with C++ expertise.

5. Perl Programming Language

Perl is a dynamic scripting language that is used quite often in networking, system administration, and website development. Knowledge of this multi-use language is a must-have for many career paths.

6. MySQL Database Management

MySQL is a database management tool that is widely used. Knowledge of MySQL is necessary for many careers, including Database Administrators, Web Developers, and Software Engineers.

7. Microsoft C# Programming Language

The C# programming language from Microsoft Corporation is rapidly gaining popularity as more companies utilize the .NET framework. It is one of the hottest career skills in the market right now for developers.

8. XML - Extensible Markup Language

XML or Extensible Markup language is a popular language that makes information on the internet view able across many different platforms. It is relatively easy to learn. While many developers know XML, fewer of them are experts in XML. It is a specialty focus that is gaining popularity for a career in web development.

9. HTML Skills

HTML continues to be a necessary skill to have for web design careers. Expert knowledge of HTML is a must-have for this career path.

10. Project Management

Management of technical projects is a necessary career skill for advancement, no matter which technical career path you choose. Formal project management training is a great start to more senior level technical roles.

Section 5

Top 10 Ways to Kick start Your Job Search

Even if you're not job searching today, it makes sense to be prepared to job hunt. You may decide it's time to say goodbye to your current job. Your employer may decide you're no longer needed. You never know for certain what might transpire at work. You might see a job posted at your dream company, and want to get your application in as soon as you can.

On average, people change jobs eleven times during their career, so it's going to happen at some point. It's better to be prepared than to have to job hunt in panic mode. It's not fun to scramble to pull together a resume at the last minute, so you don't miss out on a good opportunity.

Here are ten things you can do to help ensure you're ready to get hired.

Top 10 Ways to Kick start Your Job Search

1. Make sure your resume is current so there will be no delay if you move into job search mode. Redo your resume if the focus is on responsibilities rather than accomplishments and value added. Employers are now focusing on candidates who can generate the best results. Review resume samples and advice on updating your resume.

2. Maintain an up to date LinkedIn Profile which incorporates your latest accomplishments. Make your profile even better by including a professional head shot and examples of your accomplishments. In fact, make sure all your social pages are up-to-date, along with everything else that's visible online to prospective employers.

3. Make sure you have reference ready. to go should you need them. A good tactic is to bolster your LinkedIn recommendation and endorsements. Write recommendations for other LinkedIn contacts and endorse their skills. Some of these individuals will reciprocate or, at the least, you will feel more comfortable asking them for a recommendation.

4. Build your portfolio. It used to be portfolios were only for creative types. Employers are now eager to see work samples from professionals across the board. Put non-proprietary materials such as spreadsheets, PowerPoint presentations, press releases, and other written materials aside. When appropriate load them into your LinkedIn profile.

5. Have a professional development plan in place. Identify skills, areas of knowledge or proficiency with technology which will give you an edge in the job market. Make sure you can always tell a prospective employer about assets which you are currently developing.

6. Step up your activity with your professional association. Helping to plan a meeting or conference, working on a committee or giving a presentation are great ways to show other professionals what you can do and make contacts in a natural way.

7. Offer to help out others in your network who are in transition. What goes around comes around and you never know when you will need help. The more people you help, the more people you will have who are willing to help you when it's your turn to job search.

8. Step up mentoring activity. Find a mentor who can help you to grow or if you already have one make sure you take the time to meet periodically to get their input. Mentor junior colleagues. It will reflect positively on you and you never know when they will be in a position to give back.

9. Make sure your superiors are aware of your accomplishments. This is particularly true if you have a hands-off boss. Provide regular progress reports on your projects so they are aware of the value you are adding.

10. Do the little extra things that your supervisor likes to stay in their good graces. Offer to help out beyond your job description during crunch times. Come in early or stay late when you know it counts.

Being an exemplary employee will help you get a positive reference when you need one.

Taking some time to work on your job search each week, even if it's only a little time each week, will help you become more marketable when it's time to move on to the next step of your career.

Section 6

What to Do After a Bad Job Interview

How to Follow Up When the Interview Goes Wrong

Sometimes, no matter how much effort you put into preparing for an interview, something goes wrong. Maybe you woke up with a splitting headache or can't take your mind off a pressing personal matter. Whatever it is, circumstances may throw you off your "A game" and result in a poor performance during your interview.

Here are three strategies you can use to recover from a bad job interview.

1. Give Yourself Some Time

A bad interview can leave you feeling frustrated and upset. Take some time (whether it's ten minutes or an hour) to reflect on the experience, but don't dwell on it for too long. It's easy to spiral and become convinced that the interview went even worse than it actually did. Remember, this is only one opportunity, and there will be many more.

2. Look for Lessons

Once you've spent some time reviewing the interview, ask yourself if there is anything you can learn from your mistakes. Did the interview go poorly because you were late? Did you flub an answer to a common interview question? Did you fail to demonstrate your passion for the position? If you can identify the exact reason the interview went poorly, it can help you fix the problem, either with this position or by preparing differently for your next interview.

3. Request a Second Chance

No one wants to flub an interview, but employers are humans too and understand that people have bad days. If you think you've blown an interview, don't just give up. Although there's no sure-fire fix, it's always a good idea to send a thank you mail after your interview, and it can't hurt to explain in the note why you were off your game.

For instance, if you were feeling under the weather, you can send a thank you note saying you were feeling ill, and that it led to a poor performance that didn't demonstrate your qualifications and full interest in the position. Then, ask if there is any way you can meet a second time. Who knows, the employer may be impressed with your initiative and respect your desire to turn around a negative situation.

Asking for a Second Chance

Although not all employers have the time or resources for a "do-over," if you think you flunked an interview, take the time to email the interviewer explaining your circumstances and thanking him or her for the opportunity to interview.

You don't want to overdo your excuses, but make sure you:

- **Briefly, explain what went wrong.** For example, "I was feeling under the weather" or "I'm not typically late, but I had an unexpected childcare emergency." Keep your explanation simple and short.
- **Emphasize your interest in the job.** You can also mention the particular skills you'd bring to the position.
- **Offer to meet a second time.** Or, ask if it's an option to arrange a phone interview.
- **Reiterate the option to contact your references.** Strong references can reassure interviewers that your poor performance was atypical, and attest to your job abilities.

Here's a sample email that you might send if you find yourself in this situation.

Sample Email to Ask for Another Interview

Subject: Jane Doe Interview

Dear Mrs. Jones,

Thank you so much for taking the time to meet with me. I enjoyed speaking with you, and I feel that the position would be a great match for my academic and professional background and make use of my skill set.

However, I am not sure my interest and enthusiasm for the job came across in our interview. I have been feeling under the weather this week and don't think I was able to express my aptitude for the position.

If these things did not come across during the interview, I want to assure you that I believe my sense of initiative, high level of motivation, and positive attitude make me a prime candidate for this position.

If you have the time, I would appreciate the opportunity to speak with you again.

Also, please don't hesitate to contact my references should you have any questions or concerns about my professional performance.

Thank you again for the opportunity to interview with XYZ Company. I look forward to hearing from you.

Sincerely,

Jane Doe

Email

Phone

Section 7

How to Find Your Dream Job?

Set Your GPS - "If you don't know where you are going, any road will get you there."

In the first lesson in this series I asked you to "think different" – to approach your search as a proactive endeavor in order to tap into the millions of jobs that are never advertised.

But to do that effectively, you really need to have a clear idea of where you're going.

One of the most common job search mistakes is not defining what the ideal position looks like. Instead, most of us begin with the general premise "I need a job" and then apply for anything that we seem to be qualified for. But if you don't know the type of work you want to be doing, and the type of place you want to do it in, you will always be reacting to job descriptions you see posted online and whenever you're reacting, you're not in control.

How to take control by defining where you're going

Instead just waiting to see what gets advertised and then deciding if it appeals to you, I want you to do some real work thinking about where you want to go next. Some of the questions you might ask yourself are:

- What industries are you interested in?
- What level will you be working at? (Entry, Manager, VP)
- What department will you be in? (Marketing, Finance, Operations)
- What types of products/services the company will be selling?
- What will the culture be like? (Casual, Entrepreneurial, Structured)
- Will this be a large company, a small start-up or something in between?
- What will your day look like?

- Will you be managing others or working as a sole contributor?
- What don't you want in your next job?

Once you have defined exactly what you want to do, you get several benefits:

1. You'll be able to target your resume and cover letters and online profiles to appeal to your target audience and I'll talk more about this over the next few days. It's critically important and really makes all the difference.
2. You'll be able to focus your job search efforts by identifying companies who fit your profile and finding ways to reach them directly (more about this soon too).

Narrow your focus and you will get more interviews

If you narrow your targets from 'all the available jobs in my field or industry' to a specific sort of role within a specific sort of company, you may think you are limiting yourself, and that you will naturally get less calls and less interviews.

But actually, the opposite is true. Narrowing your focus will bring you better results. It seems counter-intuitive to say it, but it's true.

You're not right for every job

The simple fact is that you are not a fit everywhere. Every job that comes up in your field and at your level isn't right for you. The recruiters will see it when they look at your resume – and if they don't see it then, they will see it during the interview. Either way, you won't get the job and that's OK. It wasn't right for you.

A few times in my life, I've been rejected for a job that I really wanted. I was very disappointed when that happened, but in each case, I later came to realize that I wouldn't have fit in. The recruiters saw that, and the only thing that blinded me to it was how badly I wanted the job to be right.

The same is true for all of us. There are some places we fit, and some places where we would never be happy. By finding the places where you will fit, you are zeroing in on the company's most likely to respond to a candidate like you and putting all your efforts into making a positive match rather than trying to fit into the wrong shaped hole.

It's scary to narrow down your focus I know. It feels as though you're limiting your success. But try it and you'll see great results.

But what if you need a job desperately

However desperate you are, this is the right strategy. Because it's simply more effective than trying for everything with no direction in mind. If something comes along that's not ideal and you really need an income, of course you must take it, but then keep on searching for the right thing using these methods. It will work!

Be realistic

One word of warning as you develop your description of your ideal job … it must be realistic. You must have the skills and experiences necessary to achieve the goal you set. If you're not yet qualified for your dream job, then decide what the next stepping stone is, and go for that instead.

No one will decide to take a chance on an unqualified candidate, no matter how good your resume or how engaging you are in an interview – especially in this economy. Trying to make that happen is a recipe for disappointment.

What's next?

In part 3 of this series, I'm going to talk about how you can use the knowledge of your ideal position to write a focused, value-based resume. This will be crucial for a successful search, so it's important to give some thought to your ideal targets now.

By the way, I do realize a lot of what I'm saying might be different from the way you have approached your search in the past, but please do bear with me … you will see how it all falls into place as we go along. Tune in next time and you'll see what I mean!

You Owe Yourself a Career Path Plan

Career path is the process used by an employee to chart a course within an organization for his or her career path and career development. Career path involves understanding what knowledge, skills, personal characteristics, and experience are required for an employee to progress his or her career laterally, or through access to promotions and/or departmental transfers.

Career path requires an employee to take an honest look at his or her career goals, skills, needed knowledge, experience, and personal characteristics. Career path requires the employee to make a plan to obtain what is necessary for each of these areas to carry out his or her career path.

You Owe Yourself a Career Path Plan

Are you reaping the benefits of a thoughtfully developed, written, employer-supported career path plan? Creating a career path, or career path is an essential component of your life-long career management.

A career path plan is also a critical factor in performance development planning (PDP) in which a supervisor and reporting employee discuss and plan developmental opportunities for the employee. The PDP is important because it is written, shared with the supervisor, generally tracked by the organization for effectiveness, and reviewed quarterly (recommended) or regularly.

The performance appraisal, in some organizations, is also an opportunity for career path. Career path is also perceived, in organizations with a formal process, as having institutional support.

The career path encompasses both the employee's desired destination and the steps, experience, and development he or she will need to make progress on the journey. A career path gives the employee a sense of direction, a way to assess career progress, and career goals and milestones.

Developing a career path is easier, and more supported, in an organization that has a PDP process, or an effective performance appraisal or career planning process.

You can, however, as an individual employee, make your own career path plan. You are the individual for whom the career path is the most important. You deserve a thoughtful career path plan.

How to Develop a Career Path

You can develop a career path by taking a look at your desired job/jobs within your organization. Then, chart a course through jobs and departments, with the help of your supervisor or manager and Human Resources staff, that is the most likely career path that will let you achieve your goal.

Recognize that obtaining the job you desire may require lateral moves, departmental transfers, and job promotions along the way if you are to achieve your goal.

Attaining your desired goal will also require that you develop skills, pursue employee development opportunities, and obtain certain experiences as you progress along your career path through your organization.

Coaching from your supervisor and mentoring assistance from a more experienced employee, probably an employee with a position above yours on the organizational chart, will help.

Additional Considerations in Developing a Career Path

Three additional considerations exist when you develop your career path plan.

- **You need to decide on your career goals and desired jobs.** While coaching and mentoring may help you arrive at several possible career options, a complete career exploration is your own task outside of work. You can contact career professionals at your college career services offices, local community colleges, or research online where career information and career tests and quizzes abound. Dawn Rosenberg McKay offers comprehensive information about career choice and career planning.

- **Put your career path plan in writing.** If you are lucky enough to work within an organization that has an employee performance and/or career development process, the written plan is an integral component. If not, put your own plan in writing and share it with your supervisor, Human Resources, and involved others. Writing down your goals is an integral part of achieving them.

- **You own your career path plan.** You can seek assistance from others, but you are the fundamental recipient of the rewards earned by following a planned career path. You are responsible for seeking a mentor, applying for internal job openings, and developing the skills and experience necessary for you to achieve your goals. Never forget this significant fact: you own your career path plan. No one will ever care as much as you do.

How to Support Effective Career Path Planning and Development

Employees want to see and understand their next opportunities within their company. This is especially important for ambitious employees who want and expect to see career development opportunities to be satisfied and motivated at work.

A thoughtful career path plan is a key factor in employee engagement and employee retention. An organization contributes to an employee's ability to develop a career path by making the knowledge, skills, experience, and job requirements for each position within the company - transparent. With this information, the employee can plan and prepare for various jobs and opportunities.

The organization supports employees in developing and pursuing a career path by providing access to these opportunities and information.

- Job descriptions
- Job specifications
- Required competencies

- A responsive internal job application process
- Access to employees doing the job currently
- Training classes
- On-the-job developmental opportunities
- Job shadowing
- Mentoring
- Promotions
- Transfers or lateral moves
- Coaching from the supervisor
- A formal succession planning process

With access to these processes and systems, every employee should have the opportunity to pursue a career path.

How to Land Your First Job After College??

Securing that first job after college can be a daunting prospect for many college seniors and recent graduates. However, you can take charge of the process by following a few simple strategies to get your career off to a positive start.

Here are tips for landing your first job after college.

1. Check With Your Career Center

Begin by tapping the resources that are available to you as a student or recent graduate from your college.

2. Start Networking

Undoubtedly you have heard that networking is one of the most effective ways to land a job. Networking may seem difficult to you as a senior or recent graduate, so Review these career networking tips before you start.

- reaching out to contacts for information and advice rather than directly asking people to hire you.

These informational interviews will give your contacts the opportunity to gain an appreciation for your interpersonal style and your skills

3. Contact as Many People as Possible

Contact as many professionals as you can for informational consultations. Get lists of alumni volunteers from you career office or alumni association, attend networking events and ask alumni with whom you develop a rapport if you can follow up with them in the office setting to gain further insight into their work environment. Join any LinkedIn groups for your college and reach out to alumni in fields of interest.

Join professional groups in your field as a student member if you are still in college

4. Arrange a Job Shadow

When you have a positive networking meeting with someone, try to arrange a job shadow day as a follow-up.

5. Have an Elevator Pitch Ready

Take stock of your strongest interests and skills and be prepared to tell people who you meet some interesting things about yourself to grab their attention.

6. Target Your Resume and Cover Letter

As your career goals begin to crystallize, develop targeted versions of your resume. Showcase the skills, experiences, coursework, and projects most related to your emerging job objectives.

7. Find Companies You Would Like to Work For

Identify other employers of interest which are not affiliated with your college's career office to expand your options. Visit the employment section of their website and look for college student/graduate opportunities.

8. Organize Your Job Search

Get organized. Keep a database of all your applications and contacts. Schedule 10 hours per week for job searching while you are in school. Increase the time you spend to 20 hours a week during breaks and after graduation

9. Line Up an Internship

Do as many internships as possible during your college years. If you find that you are under qualified for your target job at graduation, explore the possibility of doing an internship for the summer or fall after graduation.

10. Keep Balance in Your Life

Finally, endeavor to retain some balance in your life while you are in job search mode. Exercise, follow a healthy diet, get enough sleep and continue to pursue your outside interests in order to keep your energy level up and maintain a positive state of mind.

Finding that perfect first job may take some time, but making a good match will be worth your preparation and patience.

Time Saving Tips to Speed Up Your Job Search

Sometimes it seems like finding a new job takes forever, and you can start to feel hopeless. Do you feel like your job search is off to a slow start or getting stuck? If so, read on for help getting unstuck. Here are some quick time-saving job search tips that will help your hunt for a new job go smoothly.

Be Prepared

Have a voice mail system in place and sign-up for a professional sounding email address. Consider getting a separate email account to use for your job search, so you can stay organized, and check it often. Put your cell phone number on your resume so you can follow up in a timely manner.

Be More Than Prepared

Always have an up-to-date resume ready to send – even if you're not currently looking for work. You never know when an opportunity that's just too good to pass up might come along. If you're not on LinkedIn yet, create a LinkedIn Profile and start making connections with people who can help your job search.

Don't Wait to File for Unemployment

If you've been laid-off, file for unemployment benefits right away to tide you over until you get a new job. You'll most likely be able to file online or by phone. Waiting could delay your benefits check, so look into it right away.

Get Help Without Spending Extra Cash

Utilize free or inexpensive services that provide career counseling and job search assistance such as college career offices, state Department of Labor offices, or your local public library. Many libraries provide workshops, programs, classes, computers, and printers, as well as other resources that will help you with your job search.

Create Your Own Templates

Have copies of your resume and cover letter ready to edit. That way you can change the content to match the requirements of any job you want to apply for, but, the contact information and your opening and closing paragraphs won't need to be changed. Microsoft Word users can download free templates for resumes, cover letters and email messages which can be personalized for your own correspondence.

Review Correspondence Examples and Samples

Even if you're a good writer, it's always a good idea to look at sample letters and resumes to get ideas for your own job search materials. Take a look at this collection of resume, cv, and letter samples to tailor your correspondence materials to your needs.

Use Job Search Engines

Search the job search engines to find potential openings. Use the job search engine sites to search the major job boards, company sites, associations, and other sites with job postings for you – fast. You'll be able to search all the jobs posted online in one step. You can also use Advanced Search options to find jobs that are the closest match.

Get Job Opening Notifications by Email

Let the jobs come to you. Use job alerts to sign up for job listings by email. All the major job sites have search agents and some websites and apps specialize in sending announcements. You can choose to get updates every day or less often if you prefer.

Time Savers

Strapped for time? Consider getting professional help writing or editing your resume. You'll spend a bit of money for these services, but that's going to worth the professional results.

Have Your References Ready

Have a list of three references including name, job title, company, phone number, and email address ready to give to interviewers. Print a copy of your reference list and bring it with you to interviews.

Use Your Network

Be cognizant of the fact that many, if not most, job openings aren't advertised. Tell everyone you know that you are looking for work. Ask if they can help. Be appreciative of any help they give you, even if it doesn't result in a job. You never know, they may find something for you later on.

Get Social

Utilizing social networking sites such as Facebook and Twitter can be a good way to get job listings before they are listed elsewhere. Plus, you can promote your candidacy using the social media tools that are readily available for free for job seekers. Companies are increasingly using social media for recruiting, so be ready. Here's how to get started with social networking. This tip isn't exactly a time saver, but, it will broaden your online job search resources.

Save Your Money

Paying for premium job listings may seem like a good strategy. However, before you spend your money, carefully research the site, what it offers, and how it can add value to your job search. Carefully check out the site to see what you're getting for your money. Read the fine print – some of these sites only let you cancel over the phone and charge you for a full month, regardless of when you cancel.

8 things to remove from your resume

As workplaces become more innovative and skill set requirements change swiftly, job seekers need to upgrade their skills, and more importantly present themselves accordingly. A resume is any job seeker's first impression, and this too needs to be changed – rather revamped timely –when applying for a job.

The word "Resume" or "Curriculum Vitae" or "CV" at the top of the resume

When you are applying for a job it goes without saying that you are including your resume. So do you really have to spell it out for them? Including this in heading adds no value to your application. So, first thing first, delete the heading which reads "Resume" and replace it with your name.

Objective statements

Does your resume have a generic objective statement or a rambling quote on top of it? While you think that it will add depth to your resume, the reality is that the recruiters are very well aware that your resume is written to target their jobs and that you have the skills and experience for that particular role. Stand out of the crowd by replacing the objective statement with a qualifications-based statement or introduction that highlights to the reader what you have to offer to their organization.

Hobbies

A big no to this one! Don't mention your interest and hobbies if it has no relevance to your applied job. Space on a resume is at premium, so save the space for pertinent information and use it wisely.

Work gaps

A gap in work history creates a negative reflection about your work – at least in India. While there may be valid reasons for the gap, the tendency is to think otherwise. A shorter work gap can always be discussed during the course of face-to-face interview. It's always safe, to be honest during a one-on-one conversation.

Every job you have ever had

The past experiences of your career can be collated with one line per job showing employer name, job title and dates. Try not to display every job you have ever you have done. There are chances that the last five work experiences may only be considered while shortlisting your resume. Remember, not the quantity but the quality of work done is all that matters.

Salary expectations

A pre-hand salary demand or expectation on the resume can be seen as too pesky by the employer and could be rejected on that basis. Some things can always be done off the record with smart communication.

Too much contact information

you need not display a lot of personal information. The recruiter has nothing to do with your marital status, number of kids, religion, race, country of birth, passport details etc. Your name, email address, contact number and address is all you need to share initially. For a better understanding of your professional profile, you can share the LinkedIn profile link.

References

It's important to have references from your previous job and these are checked only after you have been shortlisted for an interview. The business references do not belong on the resume unless specifically asked by the employer.

Section 9

How to Handle Taking a Career Break

Thinking of taking a career break? Whether you're staying home to care for children or traveling around the world on a year-long sabbatical, the prospect of taking extended time off from work can be equal parts exciting and terrifying. How will you survive financially while you're away from the office? And how can you make sure that your career will still be there when you get back?

The key is to do as much planning ahead of taking a career break, so that you'll be able to devote your energies to other things – plus, minimize stress when you return.

Before You Take a Career Break

Save Money

If you're reading this article, chances are that you're already biting your nails about the financial aspect of taking a break. Don't let your fear and trepidation scare you away from making practical plans.

The first step is to make a budget. How much money will you need while you're away? Think of your financial needs on a daily, weekly, and monthly basis.

Most people won't be able to bank a year or more of salary ahead of time. How much money might you realistically save? What other methods do you have for filling in the shortfall? Depending on your situation, a spouse or family member might change jobs or take on more hours, for example. Or you might decide to do some part-time work to make ends meet.

Refresh Your Network

Making the leap from a fairly stable job that you've had for a long time? Chances are that you've let your network dwindle somewhat as you gained comfort in your position. Even if you change jobs fairly frequently, it's easy to fall out of touch with former colleagues and friends.

Before you head off into the unknown, reconnect with old contacts. Plan some networking coffee dates or just a fun outing with old friends. When was the last time you went to a concert or a movie or a play? Use this as an opportunity to get motivated to make some plans. It'll be fun, plus you'll be refreshing your connections.

Have a Re-Entry Plan

Unless you're independently wealthy, you probably have an idea of when your career break will come to an end. Don't wait until then to think about how you'll get back into the swing of things professionally.

For instance, let's say you're in an industry where freelancing is common. If you're on good terms with your current employer, you might ask them if you can get in touch to pick up some contract work once you're ready.

Or perhaps you're volunteering a few hours a week during your time off. You might let it be known that you're going back to work on such-and-such a date and that you'll be looking for opportunities.

Regardless of your plans, you should keep your resume up-to-date and be ready to change your LinkedIn and other social media accounts to reflect your availability.

When You're Planning to Return to Work, Do These Things

Take Stock of Your Situation

Plans are one thing. Reality is often quite different. Perhaps you planned to be away for a year, but now five have gone by. Maybe you thought you wouldn't work at all during your time away, but you wound up taking on a part-time job. Or perhaps you left one industry only to find that for various reasons, you'd prefer to do something else when you return.

The goal now is to figure out where you are, so that you can make the transition back to work as smooth as possible.

Cope With Resume Gaps

Dealing with resume gaps can be as simple as changing resume formats or as complex as refocusing your entire CV to reflect new skills and interests.

A functional resume, for example, puts the focus on your skills and achievements, rather than on your linear work history (as with chronological resume). You can also take exact dates off your CV – this is especially helpful if you're heading back to work within a year or so of your last job ending.

There's no need to volunteer that you have an employment gap, especially if your resume does a good job of emphasizing your skills and not your chronological work history. However, you should be prepared to talk about your employment gap in a job interview, just in case an intrepid hiring manager figures out that you've been out of work.

Just remember that it's always a mistake to lie on your resume. In the first place, you're likely to get caught – and sooner, rather than later. Even if you get away with it, think of how stressful it would be to spend the rest of your career hoping that the truth doesn't come to light.

Use Your Experience to Boost Your Professional Profile

OK, so maybe you don't want to update your resume to say "Lead Domestic Engineer" (for stay-at-home parents) or "Ski Bum" (for sabbatical-takers who enjoy winter sports). But you can mine your experience outside of the workforce to improve your chances of getting a better job once you're back.

How? First of all, by giving yourself credit. Sit down and think about everything you did for the past year. Write it down in the form of a bulleted list, for easy review.

Now, tease out any and all job-related skills you acquired or developed during your time away. Did you learn a new job role at a volunteer gig? Brush up on your language or coding skills? Gain experience managing a budget? Put it in a list – and then add it to your resume.

Finally, don't forget about the friends you made along the way. Networking doesn't have to mean attending conferences or going to tedious networking events. Every person who will write you a recommendation or refer you for a job is a contact who might help you find your next big career move.

You've just spent time doing something that's so important to you, it was worth pressing pause on your career. That passion is worth something, professionally as well as personally

<u>www.oucareers.com</u>

Platform To Employment (P2E)

India's First Job Portal Who Creates Common Platform for Both Employee and Employer-Free of Cost

Oucareers Platforms are Increasingly Helping and Connect Job Seekers to Employer